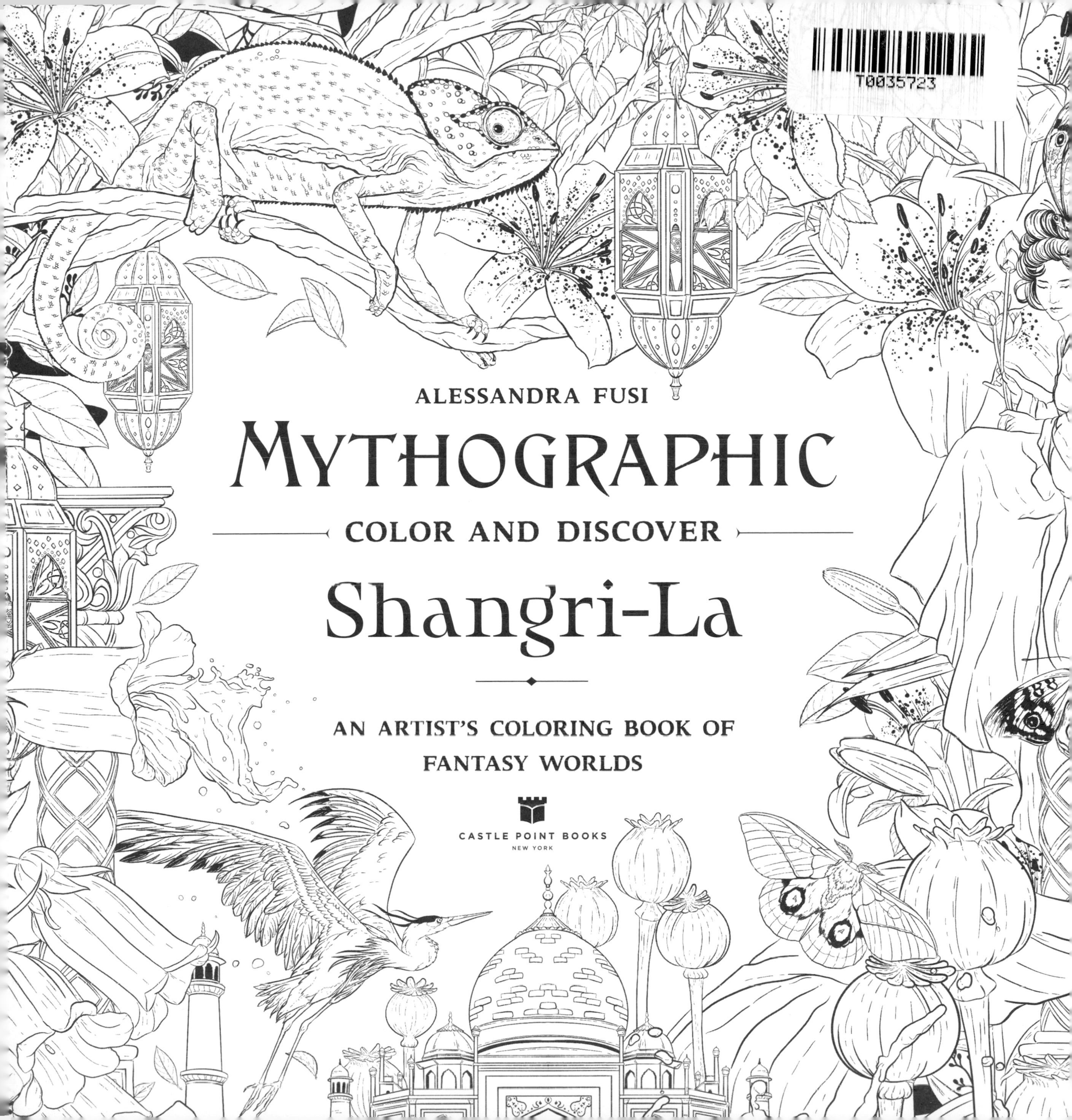

ALESSANDRA FUSI

MYTHOGRAPHIC

COLOR AND DISCOVER

Shangri-La

AN ARTIST'S COLORING BOOK OF FANTASY WORLDS

CASTLE POINT BOOKS
NEW YORK

SE
S
SW
W
NW
NE
E

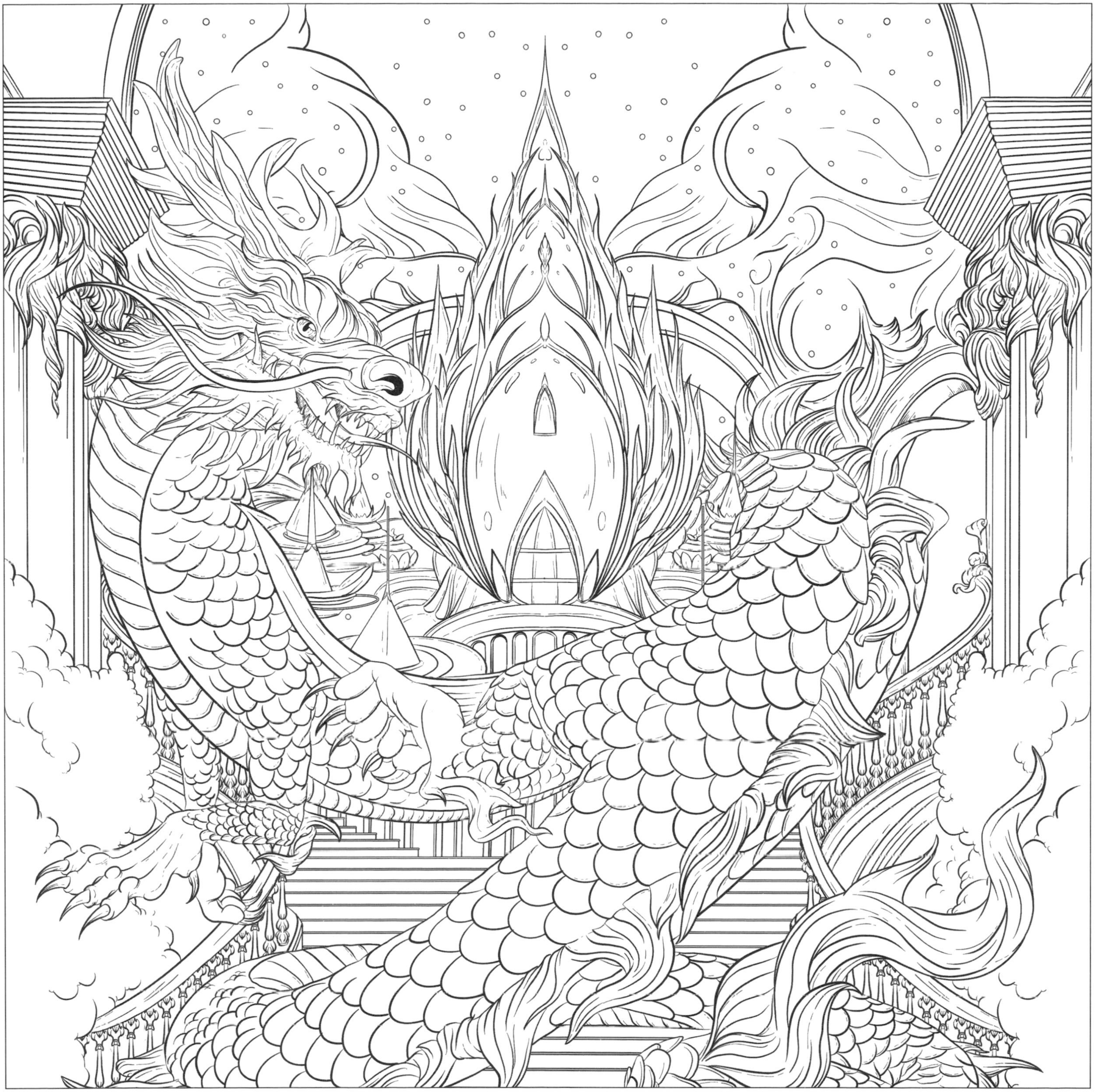

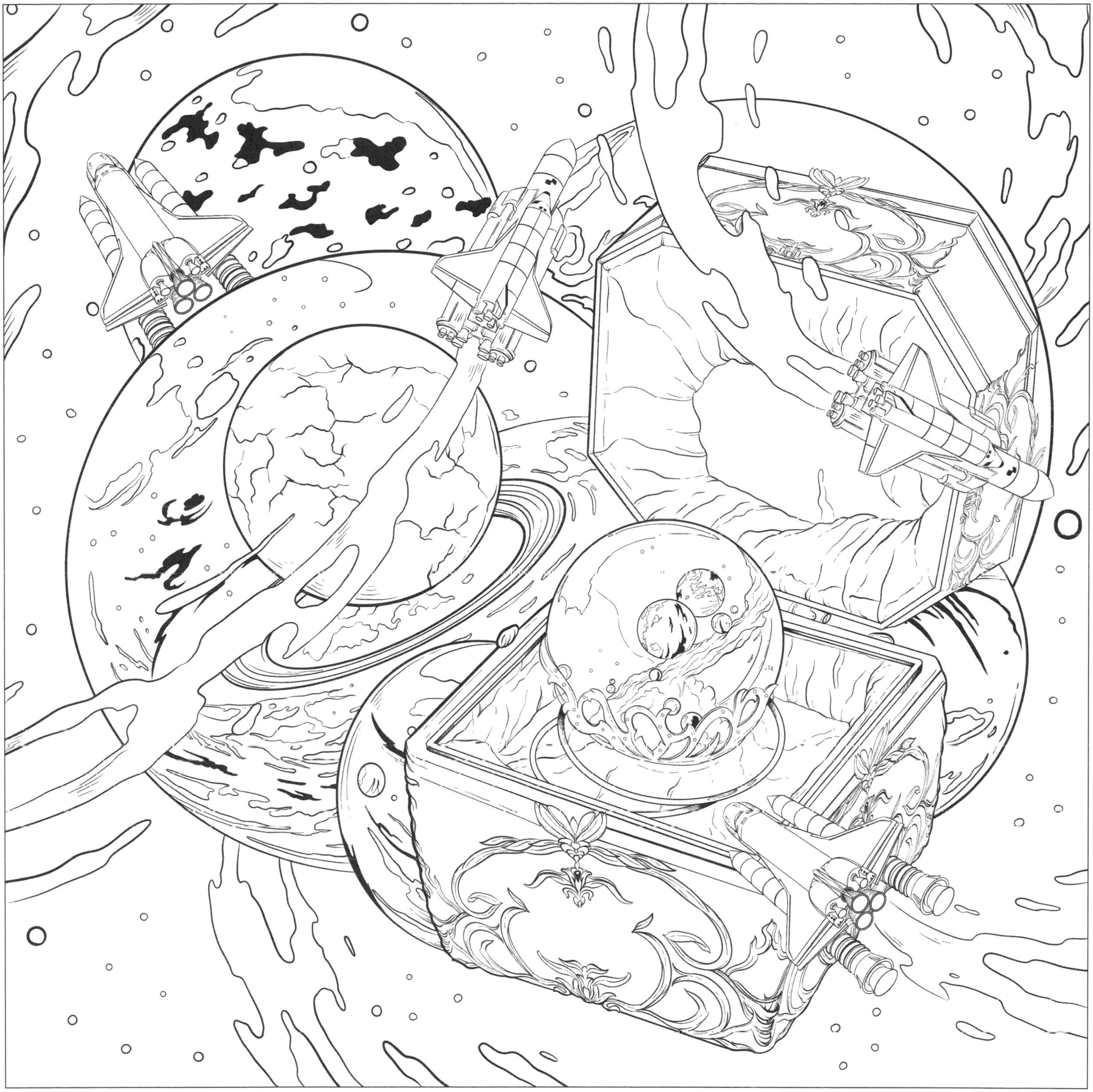

Discover more of Mythographic

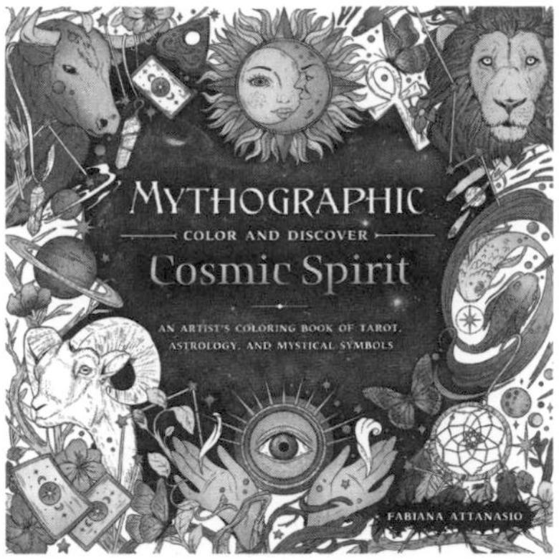
MYTHOGRAPHIC
COLOR AND DISCOVER
Cosmic Spirit
AN ARTIST'S COLORING BOOK OF TAROT, ASTROLOGY, AND MYSTICAL SYMBOLS
FABIANA ATTANASIO

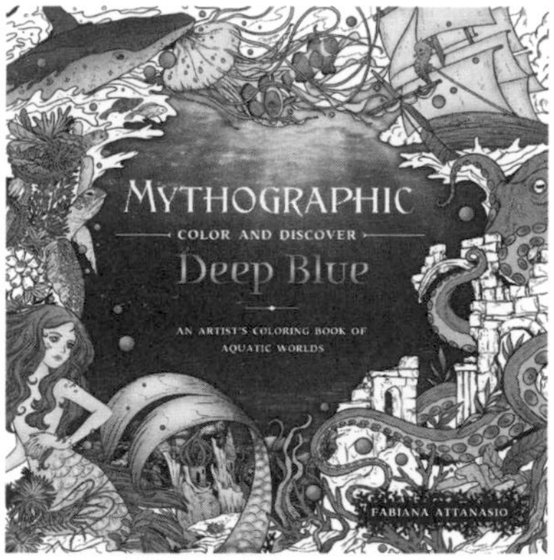
MYTHOGRAPHIC
COLOR AND DISCOVER
Deep Blue
AN ARTIST'S COLORING BOOK OF AQUATIC WORLDS
FABIANA ATTANASIO

MYTHOGRAPHIC
COLOR AND DISCOVER
Illusion
AN ARTIST'S COLORING BOOK OF MESMERIZING MARVELS
DIEGO VAISBERG

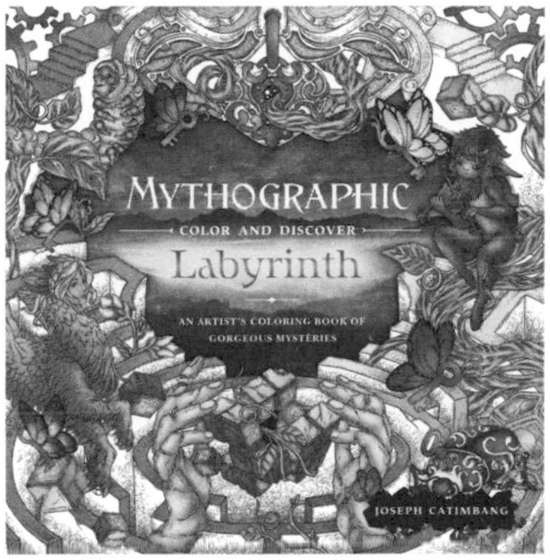
MYTHOGRAPHIC
COLOR AND DISCOVER
Labyrinth
AN ARTIST'S COLORING BOOK OF GORGEOUS MYSTERIES
JOSEPH CATIMBANG

MYTHOGRAPHIC
COLOR AND DISCOVER
Fairy Wonderland
AN ARTIST'S COLORING BOOK OF MAGICAL SPIRITS
FABIANA ATTANASIO

MYTHOGRAPHIC
COLOR AND DISCOVER
Crystal Kingdom
AN ARTIST'S COLORING BOOK OF PRISMATIC PLAYGROUNDS
WERONIKA KOLINSKA

MYTHOGRAPHIC COLOR AND DISCOVER: SHANGRI-LA.

Printed in China. For information, address
St. Martin's Publishing Group, 120 Broadway, New York, NY 10271.

www.castlepointbooks.com

The Castle Point Books trademark is owned by Castle Point Publishing, LLC.
Castle Point books are published and distributed by St. Martin's Publishing Group.

ISBN 978-1-250-32416-0 (trade paperback)

Cover design by Young Lim
Edited by Monica Sweeney

Our books may be purchased in bulk for promotional, educational, or business use.
Please contact your local bookseller or the Macmillan Corporate
and Premium Sales Department at 1-800-221-7945, extension 5442,
or by email at MacmillanSpecialMarkets@macmillan.com.

First Edition: 2024

10 9 8 7 6 5 4 3 2 1